THE BOOK OF INTERRUPTIONS

Also by Khashayar “Kess” Mohammadi

*Daffod*ls*
G (with Klara du Plessis)
Me, You, Then Snow
WJD

THE BOOK OF INTERRUPTIONS

KHASHAYAR "KESS" MOHAMMADI

A Buckrider Book

Published by Buckrider Books
an imprint of Wolsak and Wynn Publishers
280 James Street North
Hamilton, ON L8R2L3
www.wolsakandwynn.ca

Editor: Paul Vermeersch | Copy editor: Ashley Hisson
Cover and interior design: Kilby Smith-McGregor
Author photograph: Sarah Bodri
Typeset in Apertura and FreightText Pro
Printed by Coach House Printing Company, Toronto, Canada

10 9 8 7 6 5 4 3 2 1

The publisher gratefully acknowledges the support of the Canada Council for the Arts and the Ontario Arts Council. We also acknowledge the financial support of the Government of Canada through the Canada Book Fund and the Government of Ontario through the Ontario Book Publishing Tax Credit and Ontario Creates.

Library and Archives Canada Cataloguing in Publication

Title: The book of interruptions / Khashayar "Kess" Mohammadi.
Names: Mohammadi, Khashayar, 1994- author.
Identifiers: Canadiana 20250267462 | ISBN 9781998408252 (softcover)
Subjects: LCGFT: Poetry.
Classification: LCC PS8626.O4469 B66 2025 | DDC C811/.6—dc23

My "I" is too cluttered with paper.

– Hoa Nguyen

CONTENTS

Before We Begin ...

the poet's hand softens the glare of the sun
          a city   breathing
in the wake of prophets
prisoners of wars
who never learned the lingua franca
                    a thief's hand is caught
a sheikh comes to rescue with anecdotes
his worn-out sandals   a vestigium
to illuminate a passerby's mind
the witness   now bright with necessity
feeds the prisoner his last drop of water
                              and sets sail
a tower of silence
and the high priestess accustomed to blood rot
a car passes miles away   the priestess stares on
as the businessmen fall into predestination
their bucket list leading to the vagrant's cabin
bloomed crimson with the bleeding of lantern light
in the swamp nearby   the farmer's fear ripens
and breathing in the sky the martyr speaks of return
scribed in stone by the historian to persevere as material
and it is in name of the greatest insurgents we now deem tradition
that the psychoanalyst will tilt his chair and make an induction
or perhaps the ancient desire for the idol
was far too libidinal   an excess   (marked)
for the chaining of the insurgent to the gates
                    of a city   breathing
                    in the wake of poets
imprisoned in their predestination
the blacksmiths shall die blacksmiths
and the merchants shall birth merchants
during the dark hours   that abysmal volatile
the bandit jumps a fence   in the blink of an eye

becomes the pornographer of this predicament
a shadow play produced at the gates of a city
breathing
in the wake of madness
the only true heir to the divine
through the psychotic's binocular ـه
we spoke divinity   the idol
no trespasser had snatched from the maw
a cave
where Rostam slew the white deev
infinite in its capacity for madness
speaks louder than any thought that can penetrate rock
when the cavemen painted deer on these walls
they were pushing towards something unyielding
still unyielding
the psychotic assures we should pay no mind
generations wasted on mystery of death
when one does not yet know
how to hold the dagger
at the neck   of a city
that screams
and screams
and screams

Psychotic Notebooks

|

my mouth bubbling under water

the narrator mentions me by name

I am the cliffhanger

for one of a thousand nights before slaughter

having asked more questions than I have answered

in the city within the city I swerve

among the cacophony of the tunnel

an ocean within an ocean

the dung beetle on its knees

in front of a pile of shit

or the suicide hotline

and its hold music

watch out!

I am not a mountain

but the sand in your sandals years after the beach

the viral memory of an ex

fellated in darkness

once upon a time

the narrator mentioned me by name and I

was the consequence of desire

in the city of escape-artistry

||

around the lake

in the wake of the mountain

(where Farhad was sent to dig)

in the valley where nomads boil the petals for colour

there is a new framing of the sky

the absent scaffold on the carved marble

nose-chipped bas-relief of kings

a pebble has crowned the mountain

and when faced with the howl

the mountain is impersonal

shrouded in fog

in address

in city

in bludgeon

in flight

III

I can no longer afford humour

a spear knocks at my caged heart and the rattles awaken a primal fear.

a marble floor, a marble bust, all the negative space potent within rock.

mandibles in an oyster of sunlight within the sunflower. this sap.

there are things I can't do with words.

there are words that are flexed too far off the body.

clouds make way for the Alborz mountains to crack.

revealing millennia.

the sun

a temperament of the great flood.

the sun

makes new

the speech

|||||||||

I'm housed

within my own disgust

I allocate new centres

to proposed utopias

I starve myself

like a bayonet lunging forth

against the fog of war

I starve myself

to make this bread an excess

||||||||||||||

I am dressed for the poem

it doesn't take much to forge new memories

the pitch-darkness of the cradle

and the flour's ghostly shape on the ground

the nationally defined sabbath

and its afternoon boredom

wishing to be a moment on television

hushing the entire world around

||||||||||||||||

kneeling on University Avenue

a gun

and an immigration’s exit wounds

tired of bus-size projections of well-being

be right back

I have fireworks

knocking at my door

||||||||||||||||||

I have no history

my own voice whets the mirror

a political abstraction

my temperament

is a violence

to many generations to come

garments to hide your ugliness

a veil bulging at the manifest

torn at the pupil of the eye

||||||||||||||||||

death arouses the text

because the poet stays in disaster

Marx's "Permanent revolution"

to redeem all the dead as martyrs

but if I am the crowd

then why does my anger

need to recharge

if I am the crowd

then why are sensations

ingredients to violence

a generation is ample time

to rejuvenate any empty gesture

towards the tombs of the dead

a rhyming disaster

a meditative misfortune

the mountain

grief struck until it fjords

Always historicized

Or

never historicized

lost

in the lustre

of advertisement

Purgatorial Imagery

when he says he doesn't like big words
he means he doesn't like poverty

we churn in bed. a downed plane. a proxy war. we discuss. disembodied
no amount of blinking can blacken the sun. home is material.
accused of nostalgia. we correct dream grammar with a friend
as lookout. the back alleys of pleasure and that feverish night
of gender segregated discourse. my voice. still too sentimental.
a labour shortage. a company pizza party. we're heroes again.
I wake with my teeth bare. call it brain weather. no escape from the spectral.
the cold breeze. like a sadness. occulted from every cracked window.
and the saxophone that bleeds a teenage mother's exhaustion next door.
a man screams. a woman screams. a few help. most only understand.
the aftermath is a new marketing potential for water. an ice sculpture in the abyss.
we always seem to be on the precipice of a day of mourning.
the extent of our charity outreaches its intent. the hungry refuse the lamb.
the guilt-ridden are dubbed in the vernacular once a year. relative security ensues.
the fortune seller. at the mercy of the arm-hair-accented wrist.
on the street. hijab hovering without the women theorized inside.
through the bazaar they float. haggling over vegetable prices.
we announce our death prematurely to avoid pageantry.
the dust in the second-hand car's wake. a migration.
dust storms and petroleum refineries. ballistic missiles introduced at the march.
exhausted cement smoke in rural factories. Blood-thicker-than-water wars.
the upended car and its dead passengers. an uncanny intimacy with the virtual.
we are sunburnt. current like the river we won't step into even once.
somewhere in the body a limb conveys. a rush of endorphin.
and absurdity. quaking across generations of doubt.
what if we end here? raised with no-name stock disdain for the natural.
fill this void with disposable pop ephemera.
what if we end here holding hands? desiring for something.

a porous skull
a porous thought
and I am space itself
brimming with ghosts

at the precipice of the plunge
I spin into the earth's core
where I speak every language
waiting for the curtain call

"I"
an accursed transmission
ravelling and unravelling
across millennia
an archetypal blue
dysfunctional to a clear sky

when a mound of earth pearls the treasure chest
it's a redemptive coincidence
held in the womb of the house

transmission
or
translation?

"Do you want me to show you
what you want me to show you?"

we sank into the floor
caressed by the beauty
when I say my hunger is ancient
it's not for poetic effect
a century
defined in wars
so we've sold madness for bullets
but when I say I am hurting
you're caressed by its resonance with the natural
sink deeper into comfort
it is frequent   a fattening
it is a soothing
frequency

Neither big nor small enough to succeed
neither happy nor sad enough to transcend

lining props backstage,
the stagehand whispers
"there's not enough stage blood for tonight"

bored on the Machina he whinges up:
that solar monolith towering above
that matte-red star, bee-striped with ribbons of black light
that Zarathustra, floating ribbon-light
that pulsar asymptotically approaching the event horizon

and with the last ray of sunlight
we welcome hell to our city

war drums lure mothers
across the horizon
holding dead children's portraits
factory layoffs:
the bread queue lengthens
to disown us, our fathers
impregnate clouds
watch its acid rain
on our overdue homework
stomachs rug burned
papers blackening in soot
hunchbacked in the darkness
we too find happiness
in faulted walls
return to it often
in proposed homelands
terraformed in seeking
what never was

I began as a novice
to a city
long ago mastered
by the writer's eventual plunge
into blindness
the instinct to pub-crawl
came from a different breed
and the black tome of the night
painstakingly written to be fed
as an offering to the lake
as if breadcrumbs to ducks
whose soft glide
is the unfolding
of the universe

a betrayal

gods
        idols
gods
        stone
God
the parenthetical

if the high priest unsheathes the dagger
it's because sacrifice is the most economical
against a libidinous cosmology
she will fill the community pool with blood
and only let the most daring swim
in the rotten river of glory
my narrative is resolved only in the finite
no matter how many cycles the infinite repeats
its laziness comes with speculation
I too would have opinions
I too would forgo tonight's rations
I too would leave the bonfire
for a glimpse of the temporal

when the high priest blocked the path forward
it was a grand transgression

for us to be "Ancients"
we must first lose our footing
must first cease
as innovation

the martyr woke
dipped in the blood of the tulips
how obscene is death's description of the battlefield
the nation's newly redefined borders for scale
an armband, quoting scripture, drips blood
lesser than a cause   but greater
than any single instance of fire

a scorched seaside
hands clasped in prayer
at the tilt of the Milky Way above
(that dark blaze of the temporal)
((that which no one can speak to))
(((not for millennia to come)))

as the mud hardened at the footsteps of a djinn
we followed in the vestigium, climbed mountains
and found at the feet of the temple
past martyrs
prostrate
their eyes
pecked clean

the city is static
I am the buzz of its neon signs
Styrofoam dinners and
our fathers' shortcomings
in their howling intimacy
a third person was always there
hunched over at the back seat
covered in soot
we down that last swig of whiskey
to fuck in embrace of the death drive

I read THE book
on the day
of a violent mourning
the only sect with bleeding flagella
mourn behind closed doors
a phone quickly captures a violent intuition

the mourners dress their children in black
a few tears a feast

the ascetics bear the alam
– *I am a substitute*
"everybody lies"

– *I am a fake*
"perhaps"

an acceptance
a pre-emptive violence

all in due time

a prayer for the people and their unpeople
the original sin of a hemisphere
becomes prayer for
the tortured kin of another
            praise be
and *hallowed be* for a cut
the head verse
the neck verse
miserere mei, deus illiterate

safety in numbers or ...
                                    flags
the no man's land between two battlefronts
shield to shield
or perhaps an emptiness between

entire books written on warfare

not a single one

on the moment of impact

dear citizen: I am a ghost, anecdotal to a city where men weep on sidewalks

an address and the house addressed meet to beckon deer to a deer-less road: reminiscent of a disconnect between a city and a city: a disconnect of voices

my address
my form
this dungeon

dear citizen:
disturb me into the coziest centre of myself

Majnun aged a thousand years
in an instant of longing
and boys still kill themselves for love
an infatuation
counted in balconies
ambulances under the rooftop ledge
                    an eternity

we fed the fetish
she got a face full of acid
a suicide

silence is the greatest commodity
in a city that screams
and screams
and screams

we begin at bones with apparitions
what the forefathers saw shades the landscape

flesh rots and empty vessels echo
though all there is remains empty

mystics dissociate in the name of arrival
an ancient writing we can't get away from

our will breaks in absence of imminent threat
so we live in the cars our parents upended

violence that does not absolve
a city that screams
and screams
and screams

after Guy Hocquenghem, David Bowie and Brian Dedora

At the centre of it all ...
an autonomous sexuality

each man a surplus
where masculinity compounds interest

ghostly kisses
a pharmaceutical queerness

his lips smeared with fuck
as Sade dictates to the spectator

wow, beautiful hands and
failed to quote Freud

this *fatal* sodomy OR
all acts eluding reproduction

a sexuality based on deceit
this *gendered consciousness*

the utopia of the dispossessed
pilled in an eternal cuddle pile

I was entered, so I entered
I expected to be different after

in a circle for safe practice
B quotes *ribbons of cum* to constellate

a body: granted phantasy
a dream boy so angular

we can find another way
scholars still dig for meaning

all but obedience
hones the desire

At the centre of it all ...
a hole for safe practice

a map where electric wires weave to crack a blue sky

a map where sunsets foliate winter-stricken trees

a map where orange blossoms perfume the public swimming pool

a map where minds branch **Bone**/ right to **winter**

a map where the mirror stands empty
luminous only through an other

Suckling on a book
until A voice becomes THE voice
it takes time to relate to the speaker
it takes time to relate to the spoken
so I revise
well ... I can't be *the absolute*
so I might as well be myself
against a testament *so undeniable*
a poetry *so available*

we appeal to humanity
but are rejected
by blood-thicker-than-water
inherited this
sociopathy of irreverence
                this
violent ambivalence
but for the night
poetry surges
towards the free body

a phone call
drunk/high
on having never left the hustle
midway through the book I fall asleep
dream the page is disappearing

names dissipate
anonymity is key
the *good old days*
of the executioners
paid a living wage

There Needs to Be More to This Than Nostalgia

it's snowy outside my thoughts. Like *Language enriched by catastrophe* kind of snowy. I'm overcome with a callous refrain from judgment like a LONG LIVE THE PARENTHETICAL kind of judgment. when the philosopher claims the atrocity didn't happen, they say it's because he means grief is now a Jumbotron reproduction. Symbols. Simulations. Faulted walls planted underneath war manifestos. Like *Excessive generosity* kind of manifestos. My poetry was a prediction, a technique in preparation for travesty: the willow that cuts down its axe. thunder roars and I stop. *TELL THEM IT'S FOR ME.*

a poet called another poet a merchant of sugar
and we just looked at each other
cycles of holding and being held
haggling for a sound mind
the curtain offers me definition
to hell with symbols I want the real

that painting
once from a standing perspective

or Pollock
and his canvas on the floor

LONG LIVE a proclamation OR
LONG LIVE: a call to account

when I mentioned the concrete
I knew the djinn took space in the city
where I roam with my purgatorial eye
and befriend the friendliest spirits
in my fruit-flesh
seed-mouth
grape-mind
(taxonomically a psychosis)

if the pain speaks
inarticulate from atrocity
its transmission is not a moral category
but an elastic collision

LONG LIVE as a democratizing of the thinking process
move around the eyelid to shake away thoughts
I'm relative to any brighter Barzakh
my interpretive means for arrival

LONG LIVE is a personal stake in the ancient
a psyche kneeling at the helm of the sacred
I choose to read this as a journey
I choose to lead the sacred question of my mind

an echo
of a city
that screams
and screams
and screams

the wounded scream
THERE NEEDS TO BE MORE TO THIS
THAN NOSTALGIA
the voices hissing
behind a pillar at the prayer hall
wetting hands for Wudhu
you candidly uncover a nipple
>the open bathroom window
>
/that angle from which the whole city
is naked/
>
the thrusting pelvis
and its subversive metallurgy
>
the man moans and shoots
birth is an apparition
in the conception
of the may-Being

in the city that screams
my thoughts are taller than me
I'm between two hemispheres
tight-latched with worries of inflation
had it not been for rent hikes
pills woulda been tapered off
I drink my coffee
to make entertainment
of this daily news
I never moved past
that childhood anal fixation
I am queer on a curve
a race car
in traffic

I went as far as a nation

untranslated screens

and neck flesh folded over

sundried boredom

fragrant with hand-picked basil

“a cute” from “acute”

a discussed creativity in this

gentle irreverence

I went as far as a nation

but left the voice

there goes my lexicon

my mother hands me landscapes

her landscapes colour my silence

THERE NEEDS TO BE MORE TO THIS THAN NOSTALGIA

there's more to intelligence than history

beyond the mountain Qaf

through my binocular هـ

a vision

of ornamental wings

ornamental mouths

their linear incantation of prayer

when teeth weigh heaviest in the skull

I forgot the ritual

of permission

before entering a doorway

a frame

enforced

on either side of the eye

don't mind me and my struggles with the I

It mostly stems from the ache he said

and smoked the last of his cigarette

sunshine velvetly tender

I hate any warm caress

in the sour smell of underarm sweat

I crave the violence needed

for a good orgasm

the giving seed

of an apricot

Remember?

to be *something* enough

for a pronoun

Remember?

the cracked pit

of a nectarine

in childish hope

I am shaped where the city meets my anger

Polaroids, developed in the grief-shade

there's the money-named corners I'll happily trample

under any milder "Influence" of rent-transcendent reason

where we live, cock-receptacles for the nation-state

where we live, cock-receptacles

where we live, dry-mouthed, fishing for pubic hair

somehow fear can touch me
like a screen that passes through the actor

somehow my thoughts have become tangible
that bright red, bee striped in shades of opiates
where I'll flee but won't come back from for a summer

the newspapers know my predisposition
but they sell me my fix anyway
if not THE consumer then ...
an alternate consumer
of hyphenated products

the finger,
theorized in the magnetic centre of my forehead
the finger probing into my mind until it furls
touching skin

the finger
summons what I've lost

listen, I opened my lexicon to pain and it fell short of explanation

ten thousand eight hundred and thirty-seven cents owed

but in conjured hopes that the creator doesn't brag of precedence

and the creator IS that seed from which life can manifest

that single pupil that can hold the sky

my flesh consents to being a nest of insects

my consciousness is paying at the door in symptoms

Freud's retroflex, or Lacan's enjoyment of the unconscious

I'll get to the door, dancing in heels

I'll read your death in your sleep as a joyous rampage

A Harmonious Armageddon

a dance

to horror's lyricism

such

a theatrical end times

terror/ambush

goodbye to the Heimlich

the bar napkin number

and beer stench kiss

teeth clashing before kneeling

inside the stall

in harmonious Armageddon

our bodies make noise

even when our mouths

are full of sex

when tongues are wrapped

around throbbing viscera

the exam hall lover

the sex swing lover

the state-hanged lover

hips wide open

and curly haired

in my purgatorial eye

my asymptomatic love

does not wait for untied shoelaces

we put in the change

get on the massage chair

on the always-empty third floor

our eyes looking out and into the same held secret

turning backs on our ocean

is it legal to walk bare-chested

by the lake

drunk in mishearing?

I'm too tired

for their bottled beer

and rock-song toonies

blood

dried on fingertips

and blowjob eyes

telegraphed

but not acted upon

so drunk I've come out the other side

once sober/

        once drunk discussion

quoted of the Achaemenids in a BuzzFeed

quiz for my involvement in *the movement*

I have to pee

well ... I'm right here

why not just aim?

a new chapter of the Kama Sutra

My Own Private Idaho

rented but never watched

attentively enough for the discussion

a willingness to move to the US

"phone's dying" friends

I need fewer

"phone's dying" friends

we opened our lexicon to new expressions of love
the dead, waiting to be called into the coffin

I understand more and more this very routine of grief

Kant and his boring fucking ideas

Kant and his boring fucking life

I've been announced dead by a state
that was trying to kill me anyway
and when I corrected my lover's dreams
I heard buckshot rip through
the elder's face for the Amnesty cover story

Listen, I've entered knowing the risks
but have still not settled the question:
do the tortured re-emerge ready for retribution?
or does the bus leave the city limits
leaving behind but a wake of ashes?

a line stolen
from an unintended eloquence

remembering
when we were children every day

I pull aside a dreamer
who doesn't believe
in the dream
It's not the duration I say
But the rhythm of hell
and my thoughts
are kick drums
syncopated
in the purely contextual difference
between torture
and torsion
a ring of fire
OR
footsteps of the djinn
planted in wet clay

a tunnel
abandoned
before the shale

I'm walking towards the hurt
my city has a demon
my city has its own song
long lost to its greatest listeners

my city
just screams
and screams
and screams

An Autobiography

I am the age of exploration

a book written in an attempt

to force chronology

I'm still at the public bathhouse

steam, haunted by caresses

of the djinn's wedding

climbing walls to smell

orange blossoms over

still water

and the bored lifeguard

at the pool

I am the age of science books

a revised memory

a second life

in the blink of an eye

a poem written

in contempt for abolished taste-zones

I am the age of precision

a joy honed as retribution

institutionalized hopes of tame

a fear sown down

the length of my penis

the fear

of a wrong mouth

I tasted him

brined with pre-cum

knocked over the ashtray

for the kiss

I'm the age of intimacy

in bed with pain

and in pain with fear

something I'll grow

with such immediate knowledge

until death's greater teachings:

I am the age of pain

but I'll grow

that daily hurt

brick by brick

from light

I am the age of Eureka

the yard-length of a dream

counted in missed workdays

and self-care bath bombs

the rush of endorphin

when history

meets my sex

I am the age of grief

my body extends what it cannot intend

I looked back and the most-searched for

was the word "sorrow" so I'll stop

the mourners come with a presumed request

for me to keep quiet about attempts at suicide

they don't like translated grief

they want only the transmissions

so I weep and collect my tears in an egg cup

his picture at the pool, smiling

the SSRI heat exhaustion

a fox visited its copper complement

a fox

and a lack of a fox

I am the age of wounds

the dream's machinery

hope's exhaust pipe to the sky

I am the city's profoundest fear

I am the death grips of teeth on a breath

... escaping a sentence

I am the age of argument

an ex-monarch's rhetoric

applauded

as the Instagram emblem for resistance

and the flag's previous iterations

for the march against

I am the age of prayer

eyes closed for the

Closer than your jugular

the fear of bending sexwards

and catching in that reflection

a glimpse of the overseer

that *closer than your jugular*

watching me masturbate

or the *closer than your jugular*

beard that scratches my beard

I'm the age of consent

marching under banners

an AK-47 to graduate high school

a few steal bullets

others get a boot to the neck

the factory owner's son

and a forced military reassignment

closed onto the horror of dark corridors

with mother never home

empty prayer mat

and Dad's car tires crackling

on a pebble

the asphalt giving way

to my six-lane Serengeti

car tires on asphalt

headlights and shadows

crashing to the ceiling fan

like two-dimensional foam

atop the nautical darkness

wave by wave the cars

and my overseen snow-capped mount

kissing the smog halo

kissing our mouths

exhaust-smoked

to the sky

Consonants*: A Book of Visions*: A Book of Illuminations*: A Chorus of*: L*ght: Against L*ght: Against L*ght

Qaaf: think of it like the overwritten pages of a samizdat: think of it as a book: as a grimoire: think of it as a cultural movement in categorization: think of it as foldering the left behind: think of it as us floating faceless in the pre-Coca Cola times: think of us as bodies of light afloat in the age of midnight.

And then a Vowel: the window's open: words are inviting to us all with gentle patterns of light against light against light: the cosmic taxonomy where the cursed can sublimate into the sun: windows open behind where we are here and here we are delirium at the rhythm of the call.

A Vowel: language follows a certain rhythm: footsteps staggered and us still missing physical touch. from one of the ten corners of the room the word "aching" comes to mind: that face and what a face: the only face of the ONLY-face: luminous in its presence entering from the window to shine.

Alif: we're here we've been here in our delirium. we're here we've been here in this subtle longing for the language that never was. the first word: its luminous child: enters and entered and it follows and as it followed: a rhythm: frame drums syncopated in footsteps: tray after tray of sweets.

Che: we're staring: our eyes plucked from the crowd just as dusk has plucked the ONLY-face from the sky and into the silver tray of baklava. we share this delirium in the opportune moment of wind: sand still in sandals years after the beach: the invasion of the infinitesimal.

Qaaf or a Vowel: the room listens to the crowd: pure silence purifies further still. war drums syncopated in footsteps: in the wake of Damascus in the wake of our little pure water jug our little bouquet of jasmine perfuming an abandoned house: in the wake of Herodotus and his memories of the scent of Arabia.

A Vowel: we hold our original faces in our original words, touch-starved: bouquets of daffodils filling the study hall where there will soon be a lecture: a talk: our slow walk to and through the ornate hall. the ONLY-voice: recordings mention a barrage of violets and their gentle explosions behind our eyes.

Daal: it follows that there would've been more of us if we had not staggered our mass hysteria. halfway between the death drive and that oceanic feeling: Freud and Freudian still: its speed comes with rhythm and we're here: we've been here waiting for our delirium's final payoff.

Noon: The Hook: the luminous word enters and the light: our little clear water little spiritual currency: our faces are revealed in this markct of appearances: we we we and now ME that unconscious function into insight and real in the life: sentence to death: sentence: a symbol: a symptom.

A Vowel: figures in torment: runaway figures redeeming dollar-store Isaacs: the descent of language and the luminous word sat calmly at the centre of a sentence: well-guided into the lecture hall for thunder: an obvious sensation: a transubstantiation of sadness into bile.

Binocular He or a Vowel: An intricate cosmology operates without its people: our soft bodies under the rule of Mars, that ruler of Persian. The ONLY-face, its steps staggered against strips of light where faces flicker with unequivocal horror: wretched in buried inventions: wretched in body material.

The Dot Sits on a letter: we've followed the fiction of something, exceeding the explosion of light against light. why not a puddle of piss why not molasses running off of garbage bathing in the heat of the sun? why not the late-evening funk: one point perspective at the centre field taking in the expanse of material.

Vaav: manifestations and their various excreta: the economy collapses expecting the ONLY-child: the noumenology of spirit: achieving light against light. language language NOW THE INTERIOR BURSTING: there's nothing left but the outside. this liquid architecture: this impertinent uneasiness: this life perpetuated by only funk.

when the ONLY-face walks in the earth will be there: so will be the word, that pornographer of our insides: scanning layer by layer that painting: *plausible as kitchens*: our accumulated stealth: at the foot of uprooted mountains for revolutionary study: no escape from the spectral.

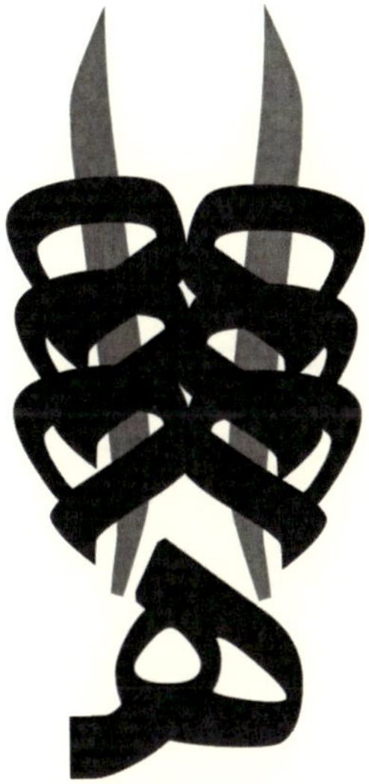

A Vowel: a hybrid biology to withdraw seeds from: what does it take to borrow a cigarette downtown? to accelerate speech to worship in it nothing but the architecture of the line: to ask the coarse canvas you can't behave like chalk. we sit to discuss poetics of the real: we end up with a fundamental dispute on vowels.

Another Vowel: from insistence to subsistence. that fikr first dhikr how a nemoone can become noumena: this commodity mysticism indentured to cosmic certainties like the entropy of light: that FIFA-approved stadium sun: that abundance of miscellany in machinery: that abundance of machinery in law.

Qaaf: to quench the thirst first quench your fetish for sugar: return to the language of milk for sweetness against wealth: curb your blood curb your thurible. curb your pretense curb your Christ. class instinction a value only in residue: this grand science of sobriety become metabolism for phenomena.

A vowel: why be nothing why be that becoming why be the very moment of WJD from existenT to existenCE why a certain monotony a certain lobotomy why be an ethical non-autonomy why a certain illusion why be deluded into the years and years and now another new year still, we lost?

Jeem: the ONLY-face imprisoned on account of being an accessory to language: language being an accessory to class curled up in that dwelling a discoloured year where death crawled into our way of being: and if not for an afternoon off and if not for dreamscapes of the ONLY-child and if not for analyses of soil and if not for analyses of fists in mud and if not for feeding the door with languaged ...

Laam: if not for a certain rhythm if not for a door: hinged on the precipice of the tongue: if not for the light occulted from that thingness and if not for the afternoon naps before and after material: if not for ladder-within-ladders if not for afternoons we reified ...

And a Vowel:

A Vowel: the ONLY-face, the ONLY-voice the ONLY-child: the ecstatic miscellany in the cum-throes of becoming: the resignation to becoming: the expanse inverted and reverted the all accredited with their stipend of the ONE.

Binocular He: let's say on our way back to consciousness, limping, sex calls but sex is the quietest sound: a voice different from the mouth: birthed and carried to term. the difference between horizontal, and vertical thoughts, where light tickles the scalpel can pry: sound scatter over field recordings of Montreal.

Another Vowel: and light again, yellowed and blued and bright in fire. the dandelion that lonesome *Messenger* from Q-S-D to Q-aa-S-i-D-ak where the *Messenger* Ex-Tends what it cannot IN-Tend. that if I sat with it and paid attention, that considering the overwhelming radiation of matter into light: that if that duality between matter and energy made its original flight:

A vowel: that hydraulic hiccup: the hydro-sonic growl: *mine mine* oh wait my mister called. an inch of cold water for rice measured in fingertips. new-found poetics in misheard first-date convos: a first date consensual clause made the clattering loss of dignity for the ONLY-ear and its dissonant yet shattering minds.

And another Vowel: I owe to Sheitan my every single design: oh fear so umbilical: Germanic and haunted in degenerative loops and dark reverberation of loss: there is the bright sheen of fire but what we see is only obsidian smoke rising to chip by chip cut the sky.

And another Vowel: an impression of butter on burnt toast: an impression of Christ against rock. fear is a purely acoustic enterprise. neurons blunt in the sudden insurgence of the ONLY-thought: knives dulled and red streaks reflected off each glass of wine: a prophecy for outlived viscera:

And another Vowel: I can't listen because I keep creating fictions. fictions keep crashing. to wash television. to wash minds. "Water," "Bird" only syllables when placed in a clay pot. the notion-state of failure and the nation of the past.

Vaav: and a Vaav: and a Vaav: and another Vaav: the comb lit up. follicles blossomed. dulcimers were laid down to rot. a foretold history where no future is an epoque. a designated return where no light is dealt in exchange for the ONLY-sun. a word, then a word then anger. a word salad a word sandwich. a language crashing at the heat of the sun.

ACKNOWLEDGEMENTS

This manuscript would not have been possible without the mentorship of Rahat Kurd and Zoe Imani Sharpe. I'd like to thank the Chalmers Professional Development grant for allowing me to seek mentorship with such amazing artists.

Great thanks to Bianca Stone for shaping an early version of this manuscript.

More than anything, this manuscript is inspired by the scholarship of Jason Bahbak Mohaghegh and his many fantastic lectures from The New Centre for Research and Practice.

I'd like to thank the Canada Council for the Arts, Ontario Arts Council and Toronto Arts Council for funding this manuscript.

Poems from this manuscript have appeared in *Iterant, The Ex-Puritan, The Sprawl Mag, Matter, The Ampersand Review, Prism International, Contemporary Verse 2, The Malahat Review, Filling Station* and *Plenitude Magazine.*

Many thanks to Paul Vermeersch and Noelle Allen for bringing this book to life.

Khashayar "Kess" Mohammadi (they/them) is a queer, Iranian-born, Toronto-based poet, writer and translator. They are the winner of the 2021 Vallum Poetry Award and the author of nine chapbooks of poetry. *The Book of Interruptions* is their fifth poetry book.